W9-BWF-473

DATE DUE

Arbor Day

Mir Tamim Ansary

Heinemann Library
Chicago, Illinois

C1   2003   14.95

Customer Service 888-454-2279
Visit our website at www.heinemannlibrary.com

Designed by Depke Design
Printed and bound at Lake Book Manufacturing

06 05 04 03 02
10 9 8 7 6 5 4 3 2

Library of Congress Cataloging-in-Publication Data
Ansary, Mir Tamim.
   Arbor Day / Mir Tamim Ansary.
      p. cm. -- (Holiday histories)
   Includes bibliographical references (p.   ).
   ISBN 1-58810-219-X
   1. Arbor Day--United States--Juvenile literature. [1. Arbor Day. 2.
Holidays.]   I. Title.
   SD363 .A62 2001
   394.26--dc21

                                    2001000069

Acknowledgments
The author and publishers are grateful to the following for permission to reproduce
copyright material:
Cover photograph: Tony Stone
p. 4 Brenner/Photo Edit; p. 5 David Young-Wolff/Photo Edit; p. 6 Richard Kolar/Earth Scenes; p. 7
Myrleen Ferguson/Photo Edit; p. 8 David David Gallery, Philadelphia/SuperStock; pp. 10, 11, 12, 14,
16 North Wind Pictures; pp. 13, 15, 17, 18, 19 The Granger Collection; p. 20 Underwood Photo
Archives; p. 21 Hans Reinhard/Bruce Coleman, Inc.; p. 22 AY Owen/Time Pix; p. 23 SuperStock;
p. 24 Will & Deni McIntyre/Photo Researchers; p. 25 Bill Aron/Photo Edit; p. 28 Paul Conklin/Photo
Edit; p. 29 Photo Edit.

Every effort has been made to contact copyright holders of any material reproduced in this book.
Any omissions will be rectified in subsequent printings if notice is given to the publisher.

Some words are shown in bold, **like this.** You can find
out what they mean by looking in the glossary.

Contents

A Day for Trees

It is a cool day in late April. It looks like it might rain today. Why are these children outdoors? Because their school is celebrating Arbor Day.

Arbor comes from an old word that means "tree." People celebrate Arbor Day by planting trees. These children are planting a peach tree.

Arbor Day in the Past

Arbor Day is not well known today. But 50 years ago, it was very popular. Your grandparents may have planted trees on Arbor Day.

Why is there a special day for trees? Why not a Grass Day? Why not a Bush Day? Let's look at how this day started.

Forests and Plains

Five hundred years ago, North America had huge forests. They covered both the East and West **coasts.** In the north, forests stretched from ocean to ocean.

The middle of the continent had few trees. This huge flat area is called the Great Plains. At one time, this area was mostly covered by tall grass.

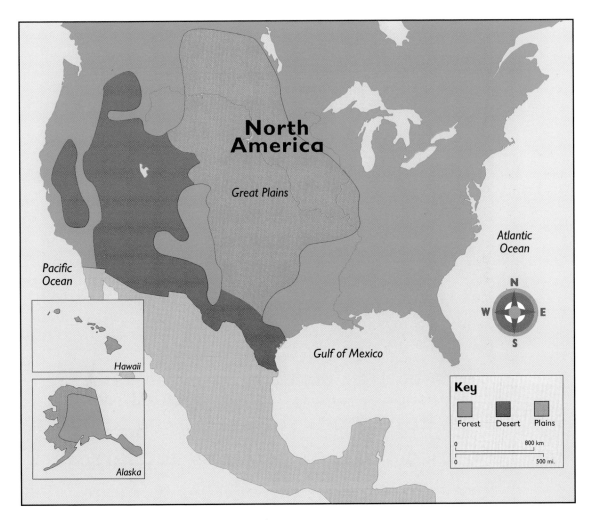

North America

Great Plains

Pacific Ocean

Atlantic Ocean

Hawaii

Alaska

Gulf of Mexico

Key

Forest   Desert   Plains

0   800 km

0   500 mi.

N
W   E
S

Enter the Europeans

Then **Europeans** started moving to North America. Many of these new **settlers** were farmers. They cut down trees to make room for **crops.**

As more settlers came to North America, people kept moving west. They kept cutting down trees and planting crops. But when they reached the Great Plains, they slowed down.

A Land Without Trees

The **settlers** did not think they could live on a land with few trees. How would they build houses there? How would they make fires in the winter?

Also, the plains are very hot in summer.
With few trees, where would shade come
from? The settlers called these plains the
Great American Desert.

Crossing the Plains

Some brave **explorers** crossed the plains. They came back with stories of good land on the other side. Soon others crossed the plains, too.

They traveled in groups of covered wagons. They made their way to Oregon and California. Only a few stopped to live on the plains.

Settling the Plains

Settlers on the plains built houses out of **sod.** They planted **crops.** They got plenty of water from rain. The plains were a good place for farming after all!

★
16

One of the early settlers was a man named
J. Sterling Morton. He and his wife moved
to Nebraska from Michigan in 1854.
Morton wanted to start a newspaper.

The Railroad

In the 1860s, a railroad was built across the country. After that, people could live on the plains more easily. They could get their **supplies** by train.

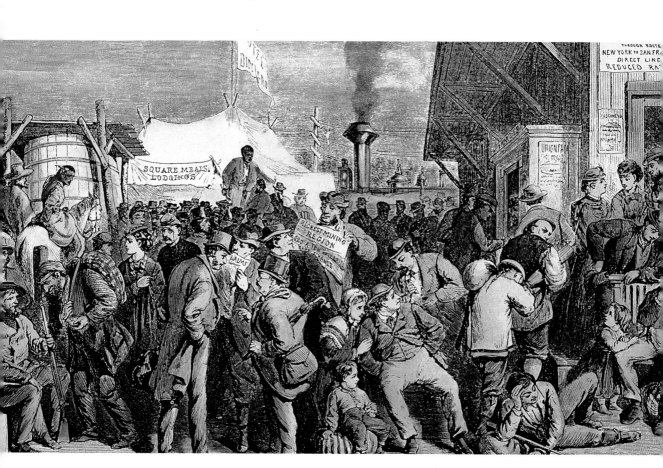

They could also send **products** to **market** by train. So, more people moved to the plains to farm or **raise cattle.** Towns and cities quickly formed.

★

The Importance of Trees

By this time, J. Sterling Morton was running Nebraska's first newspaper. He often wrote about his love of trees. He pointed out their importance.

Morton wrote that trees give us more than wood and fruit. Their roots keep soil from blowing away. In a windy place like Nebraska, he said, farmers need trees.

Arbor Day Is Born

Morton planted about 300 trees on his own land. He asked others to plant trees, too. In 1872, he came up with the idea of Arbor Day.

He asked that everyone in Nebraska plant
trees on April 10. The people of Nebraska
liked Morton's idea. They planted more
than one million trees that day!

★

An Idea Spreads

Morton's idea spread. Soon, schools were setting aside a day for planting trees. The idea moved to other countries as well.

For example, Arbor Day is now popular in Israel and Australia. Both countries have big deserts. Trees have made these deserts nice places for people to live.

Jerusalem, Israel

Tomorrow's Trees

Today, our forests are getting smaller. We are cutting down trees to make paper and **lumber.** But we do not have to run out of trees. We can plant more.

Redwood trees, California

Arbor Day is about the future. If you plant an apple tree today, your children may enjoy the fruit. Or suppose you plant a redwood. It may be standing 1,000 years from now!

★
27

Arbor Day in Your State

Alabama – Last full week in February

Alaska – Third Monday in May

Arizona – Last Friday in April

Arkansas – Third Monday in March

California – March 7-14

Colorado – Third Friday in April

Connecticut – April 30

Delaware – Last Friday in April

District of Columbia – Last Friday in April

Florida – Third Friday in January

Georgia – Third Friday in February

Hawaii – First Friday in November

Idaho – Last Friday in April

Illinois – Last Friday in April

Indiana – Last Friday in April

Iowa – Last Friday in April

Kansas – Last Friday in March

Kentucky – First Friday in April

Louisiana – Third Friday in January

Maine – Third full week in May

Maryland – First Wednesday in April

Massachusetts – April 28-May 5

Michigan – Last Friday in April

Minnesota – Last Friday in April

Mississippi – Second Friday in February

Missouri – First Friday in April

KEY		
November	December	January
February	March	April	May

28

Every state now has an Arbor Day, but not on the same date. That is because the best time to plant trees is not the same in every state. This chart shows when Arbor Day is observed in each state.

Montana – Last Friday in April

Nebraska – Last Friday in April

Nevada – Last Friday in April

New Hampshire – Last Friday in April

New Jersey – Last Friday in April

New Mexico – Second Friday in March

New York – Last Friday in April

North Carolina – First Friday following March 15

North Dakota – First Friday in May

Ohio – Last Friday in April

Oklahoma – Last full week in March

Oregon – First full week in April

Pennsylvania – Last Friday in April

Rhode Island – Last Friday in April

South Carolina – First Friday in December

South Dakota – Last Friday in April

Tennessee – First Friday in March

Texas – Last Friday in April

Utah – Last Friday in April

Vermont – First Friday in May

Virginia – Second Friday in April

Washington – Second Wednesday in April

West Virginia – Second Friday in April

Wisconsin – Last Friday in April

Wyoming – Last Monday in April

Important Dates

Arbor Day

1607	**Settlers** from England start coming to North America
1841	People start crossing the plains on the Oregon Trail
1854	J. Sterling Morton moves to Nebraska
1866	Work on the first railroad across the country begins
1867	Nebraska becomes a state
1869	The first railroad across the country is completed
1872	The first Arbor Day is observed (April 10)
1874	Nebraska sets April 10 as the date for Arbor Day
1882	Schools across the country begin celebrating Arbor Day
1885	Nebraska sets the last Friday in April as the date for Arbor Day

Glossary

cattle cows, bulls, and calves

coast land near an ocean or sea

crops plants grown by farmers for food and other uses

Europeans people from the continent of Europe

explorers people who travel to new places to see
  what is there

lumber wood sawed into boards

market place where products are bought and sold

products anything made, grown, or raised to be sold

raise to feed or take care of animals

settlers people who move to a new place to live

sod block of soil held together by grass roots

supplies things needed by humans

More Books to Read

Ayers, Patricia. *A Kid's Guide to How Trees Grow*. New York:
  PowerKids Press, 2000.

Iverson, Diane. *My Favorite Tree: Terrific Trees of North America*.
  Nevada City, Calif.: Dawn Publishing, 1999.

Schwartz, David M. *In a Tree*. Milwaukee, Wis.:
  Gareth Stevens, Inc., 1999.

Index